When Things Are Different

Written by: Runda Ebied
Illustrated by: Eman Salem

Copyright © 2020 by Runda Ebied

All rights reserved.

ISBN: 978-1-7773037-0-9

No part of this publication may be reproduced in whole or in part, or stored in a retrieval system or transmitted in any form or by any means, electronic, mechanical, photocopying, recording, or otherwise, without written permission of the author.

Dedicated to my children, who inspired me to write this book and to all the children around the world, coping with changes– you are brave, you are resilient, you are loved.

Sometimes when things are different,
I have trouble with how to cope.
I try to see the bright side,
To keep going with a sense of hope.

Hope that things will get better,
And that I'll feel good again.
It helps me to close my eyes and breathe,
And count from one to ten.

Sometimes things are different,
When we move to somewhere new.

And we try to get used to the changes,
While finding a new friend or two.

Sometimes things are different,
When we can't see our family and friends.

Sometimes people are sick or move away,
I really don't like goodbyes and ends.

Sometimes things are different,
When our family deals with a change.

When things are really different,
As we start a new school year,
With new teachers and new classmates,
We can feel worry and fear.

When I'm feeling nervous,
And wish for things to be like before,
I'll remind myself of how brave I am,
And I can get through this, I'm sure.

Sometimes things are different,
When we have to follow new rules.

To keep everyone safe and healthy,
At stores, parks, and schools.

When things are different and we feel scared,
It's really important to know,
We've gone through other changes before,
And we'll deal with this one, we'll take it slow.

I'll name my fears and talk about them,
To the people I love and hold dear,
We'll come up with ways to feel better,
Until my worries and fears disappear.

When I'm feeling afraid because things have changed,
I put my hand on my heart.
I think of things that help me feel better,
And get ready for this new start.

When things are really different,
To myself I will always say,
Hard times don't last forever,
And things will get easier someday.

About The Author

Runda Ebied is a mother of two children, and an Occupational Therapist by profession. Throughout her career, Runda has worked with individuals with mental health difficulties, as well as children with special needs both in school settings and within children's homes. Runda is very passionate about maternal mental health and children's emotional and mental well-being.

Runda has an online platform on Instagram and Facebook dedicated to these important topics: @mothercarejourney and more of her writing can be found on www.mothercarejourney.com

www.ingramcontent.com/pod-product-compliance
Lightning Source LLC
Chambersburg PA
CBHW051307110526
44589CB00025B/2965